Lyndon B. Joh

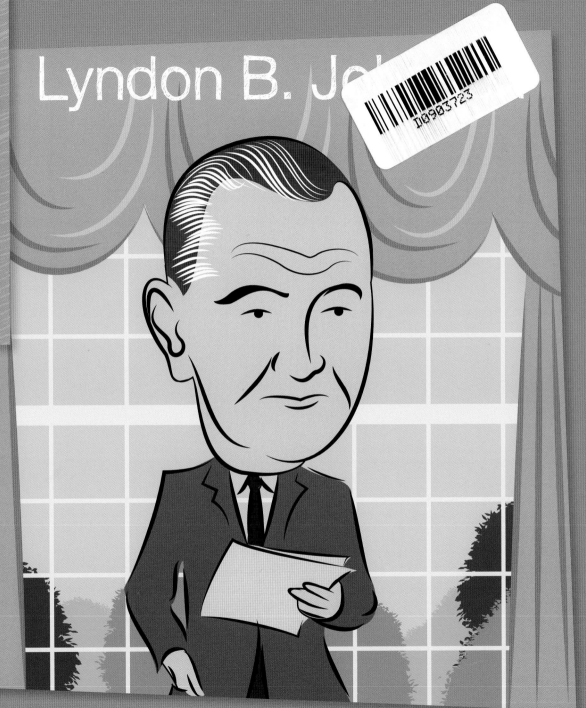

Published in the United States of America by Cherry Lake Publishing
Ann Arbor, Michigan
www.cherrylakepublishing.com

Content Adviser: Ryan Emery Hughes, Doctoral Student, School of Education, University of Michigan
Reading Adviser: Marla Conn MS, Ed., Literacy specialist, Read-Ability, Inc.
Book Design: Jennifer Wahi
Illustrator: Jeff Bane

Photo Credits: LBJ Library by Unknown [ca. Early 1909] / Serial No. 09-3-3/ Public Domain, 5; LBJ Library by Unknown [ca. 1928] / Serial No. 28-13-1/ Public Domain, 7; © Kamira / Shutterstock.com, 9, 22; LBJ Library by Unknown [1934/1935] / Serial No. 34/35-13-1 / Public Domain, 11; © Everett Historical / Shutterstock.com, 13; LBJ Library by Unknown [May 3, 1941] / Serial No. 41-5-12 / Public Domain, 15; LBJ Library by Unknown [March 1942] / Serial No. 42-3-7 / Public Domain. 17; LBJ Library photo by Cecil Stoughton [November 22, 1963] / Public Domain, 19, 23; Photographed by Thomas J. O'Halloran [September 1955] / Library of Congress, 21; Cover, 1, 8, 16, 18, Jeff Bane; Various frames throughout, Shutterstock.com

Library of Congress Cataloging-in-Publication Data

Names: Devera, Czeena, author.
Title: Lyndon B. Johnson / Czeena Devera.
Description: Ann Arbor : Cherry Lake Publishing, [2017] | Series: My
  itty-bitty bio | Includes bibliographical references and index. |
  Audience: Grades K-3.
Identifiers: LCCN 2016056244| ISBN 9781634728171 (hardcover) | ISBN
  9781634729062 (pdf) | ISBN 9781634729956 (pbk.) | ISBN 9781534100848
  (ebook)
Subjects: LCSH: Johnson, Lyndon B. (Lyndon Baines), 1908-1973--Juvenile
  literature. | Presidents--United States--Biography--Juvenile literature.
Classification: LCC E847 .D52 2017 | DDC 973.923092 [B] --dc23
LC record available at https://lccn.loc.gov/2016056244

Printed in the United States of America
Corporate Graphics

table of contents

My Story 4

Timeline. 22

Glossary 24

Index 24

About the author: Czeena Devera grew up in the sweltering heat of Arizona surrounded by books, quite literally as her childhood bedroom had built-in bookshelves constantly overflowing. She now lives in Michigan with an even bigger library of books.

About the illustrator: Jeff Bane and his two business partners own a studio along the American River in Folsom, California, home of the 1849 Gold Rush. When Jeff's not sketching or illustrating for clients, he's either swimming or kayaking in the river to relax.

I was born in 1908. I grew up in Texas.

We lived on a farm. We were poor.

I did not do well in school.
But I liked public speaking.

I became a teacher. I taught
poor people. I wanted to help
them.

I worked for a member of **Congress**. I liked my job.

Who would you like to help? Why?

I married Claudia Taylor.
Her nickname was "Lady Bird."

I loved my family.

Do you have a nickname?

I helped young people find jobs and education.

I became a member of Congress.

I was well liked. I served many **terms**.

The United States entered **World War II**. I **volunteered** in the war. I was brave. The military honored me.

I was President John F. Kennedy's **vice president**. But he was killed. I became the 36th president. I helped calm the nation.

I did not run for president again. We had many problems. I could not solve them all.

I died in 1973. I wanted the best for our nation.

What would you like to ask me?

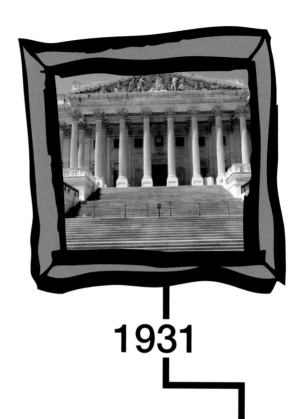

1931

1900

Born
1908

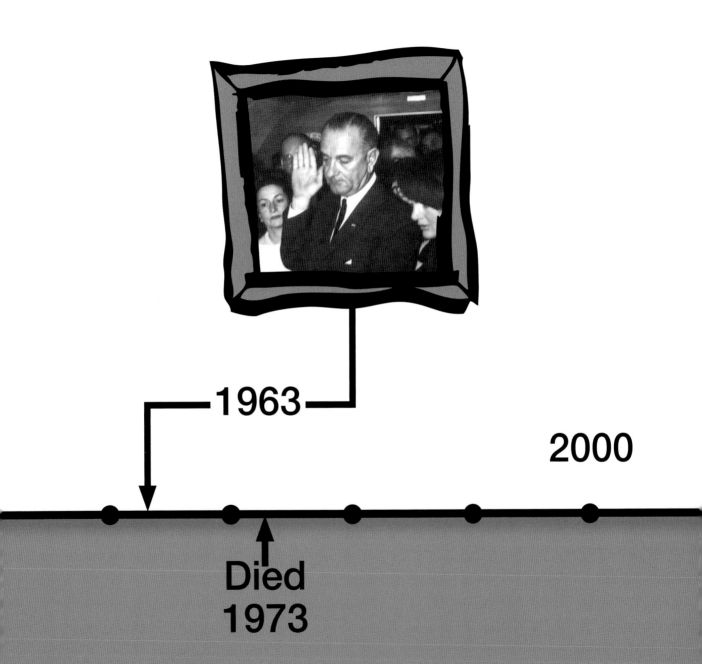

1963

2000

Died
1973

23

glossary

Congress (KAHNG-ris) the lawmaking body of the United States

terms (TURMZ) periods of time, such as years

vice president (VISE PREZ-ih-duhnt) the person who is next in power after the president

volunteered (vah-luhn-TEERD) offered to do a job without pay

World War II (WURLD WOR TOO) a war fought overseas from 1939 to 1945

index

Congress, 8, 14

military, 16

nation, 18, 20
nickname, 10-11

poor, 4, 6
President John F.
    Kennedy, 18
president, 18, 20
public speaking, 6

school, 6

teacher, 6
term, 14
Texas, 4

World War II, 16